ACTION CONTRAPTIONS
Easy-to-Make Toys that Really Move

by Mary Blocksma and Dewey Blocksma

illustrated by Sandra Hulst

Prentice Hall Books for Young Readers
A Division of Simon & Schuster Inc.
New York

Published by Prentice Hall Books for Young Readers,
A Division of Simon & Schuster Inc.
Simon & Schuster Building
Rockefeller Center
1230 Avenue of the Americas
New York, NY 10020
PRENTICE HALL BOOKS FOR YOUNG READERS is a trademark
of Simon & Schuster Inc.
Designed by Constance Ftera
Manufactured in the United States of America

10 9 8 7 6 5 4 3 2 1

Library of Congress Cataloging in Publication Data
Blocksma, Mary
    Action contraptions.
    Summary: Presents instructions for making
cars, trucks, and other toys out of materials
found around the house.
    1. Toy-making—Juvenile literature.
[1. Toymaking. 2. Handicraft] I. Blocksma,
Dewey. II. Hulst, Sandra, Ill. III. Title
TT174.B55 1987   745.592   87-2295
ISBN 0-13-003352-9

To Carol Barkin,
our tireless editor,
with thanks and cheers

TABLE OF CONTENTS

BECOME A TRANSFORMER!

You're not going to believe how you can transform junk and inexpensive materials into amazing action toys that really move! In minutes, you can transform a balloon into a Ping-Pong Popper, a plastic coffee can lid into a top, gumballs into racers, cups into wind spinners, plumbing insulation into authentic-looking tires and cars.

You're about to find out that ho-hum materials are much more than what they seem. A Styrofoam plate is more than a plate—it's a top, or a floating ring, or the wheels on a toy car. A plastic soda pop bottle is not just a container—it's a racer body or a drum. And a picnicware cup holds more than juice—it can also hold the wind.

Gather the tools and some of the materials on the next page, and start building. After you've made some of the toys in this book, think up some more action contraptions on your own!

WHAT YOU NEED

Tools

a strong pair of scissors
a pencil
a paper punch

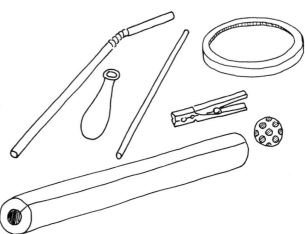

Materials

You will find most of the things you need at a general or discount store that has a hardware department or at a hardware store. Be sure to ask someone to help you find what you need.

Styrofoam plates (the cheaper, the better!)
practice golf balls (plastic ones with holes), or Ping-Pong balls
2 ⅛-inch diameter wooden dowels
2 ¼-inch diameter wooden dowels or some Tinker Toy sticks
round balloons in assorted sizes
plastic straws
1 3-foot length of foam pipe insulation (from a hardware plumbing department)—the kind with the smallest center hole works best

Other materials can be found around the house:

plastic lids	white glue
marbles	shoe boxes or other small boxes
crayons	toothpicks
clamping clothespins	plastic soda pop bottles
plastic tape (black electrician's tape works fine)	

PLAY IT SAFE

Of course you'll use your good sense when you make and play with the toys in this book—but it doesn't hurt to be reminded.

1. The toys in this book are not baby toys. Don't let children under five play with them.
2. Don't ever eat candy or gum that others have handled or that you have made into toys.
3. Remember that scissors have sharp points—keep them pointed away from yourself and other people.

JAZZ UP YOUR CONTRAPTIONS

It's worth taking a little time to make your toys look good. A few bright additions give fantastic pizzazz to almost any action contraption. If poster paint won't stick—it only works on paper and wood—try attaching some of these to your contraptions:

brightly colored plastic tapes
bright plastic throwaways, like bread wrapper closers, bottle caps, little toys, etc.
permanent felt markers (Be careful—they can stain clothes!)
crayoned designs
stickers
your own racing flags

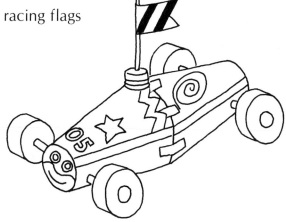

HOW TO MAKE RACING FLAGS

Flags aren't just for cars. Once you get going, you'll want to put them all over the place—on your pocket, atop a wind toy, on the door of your room, on your bike, above your bed!

What You Need

flag material: paper, white or printed (gift wrap makes great flags), or a bright scrap of cloth
flagpole: a toothpick for a small flag; a wooden dowel, pick-up stick, or plastic straw for a bigger flag
scissors and white glue

What You Do

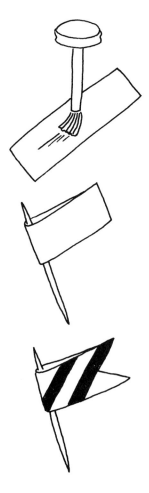

1. From paper or cloth, cut a strip as wide as you want your flag to be, but at least twice as long.

2. Fold the strip in half. Open it. Spread glue on the wrong side. Fold the flag over the stick.

3. Trim the flag to any shape you want—triangle, fish, rectangle, whatever. If it's plain, paint or glue a design on each side.

MINUTE MITES

Let's start with three easy toys you can make in just minutes.

PING-PONG POPPER

You won't believe how far this small ball will go!

What You Need

1 small round balloon
1 Ping-Pong ball or practice golf ball

What You Do

Blow the balloon up to about the size of a lemon or orange—no bigger. Knot the end.

How It Works

Press the ball into the balloon with both hands. Slide your fingers off and—*kapowee!*

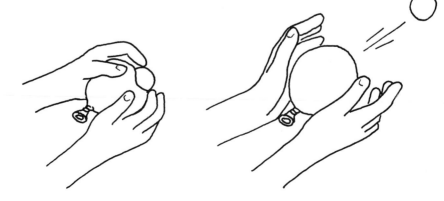

PONG PONG DRUM

It looks like a rattle—sounds like a drum!

What You Need

1 largish round balloon
1 Ping-Pong ball
1 small plastic soda pop bottle
plastic tape

What You Do

1. Cut the top off the balloon,
   below the neck.

2. Cut the bottom off the bottle.
   Hold the bottle, bottom up,
   between your knees. Put the
   Ping-Pong ball in the bottle.

3. Use both hands to stretch the
   balloon tightly over the bottom of
   the bottle. Tape it in place.

How It Works

To play the drum, shake the bottle.
Change the tone by holding your
hand over the open end.

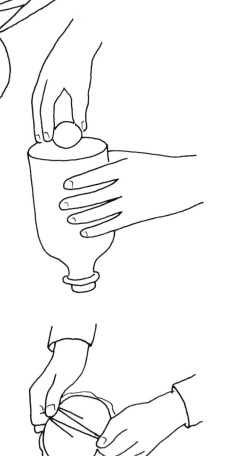

ROOM RING

This feather-light floater flies indoors—it even bounces off walls!

What You Need

scissors

1 Styrofoam plate (Some brands of Styrofoam plates won't work. The lighter and flatter plates work best.)

What You Do

1. Cut out the middle of the plate a little above the curve. This inner circle will become your Room Ring.

2. Now cut the center out of your circle. The rim should be this wide <——————> (about 1 inch) all the way around. Don't cut through the ring!

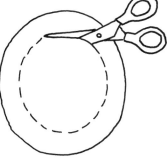

How It Works

To fly the Room Ring, fling it gently like a Frisbee. If it doesn't glide nicely, trim a *tiny* bit off the outside or a *tiny* bit off the inside. Or snip around the inside and gently push the inner edge down.

SPINNERS

Make a batch of toys to spin in the air, on the table, or on the floor! Some are quick, some are crazy, but they're all great fun.

MINI SPINNER

Use a practice golf ball if you can—it has holes in it already. If you're using a Ping-Pong ball, you might want to ask an adult to poke the holes.

What You Need

1 practice golf ball (or Ping-Pong ball)
1 plastic straw   plastic tape   scissors

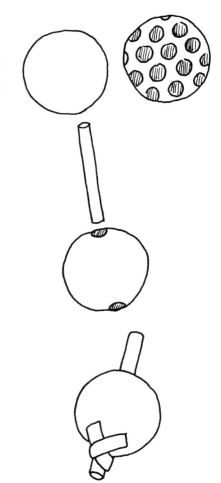

What You Do

1. If you're using a Ping-Pong ball, poke a straw-sized hole in the top with a scissors. Poke another hole directly opposite the first one.

2. Cut the straw in half. Poke the half *without* the bend through the holes in the ball far enough to make a short tip.

3. Cut a piece of tape in half *lengthwise* and twist it around the tip end of the straw. Attach the tape-ends to the ball.

How It Works

Twist the handle of the Mini Spinner between your fingers and drop it on a smooth surface.

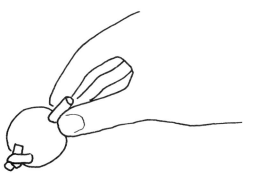

INSTANT TOP

You probably won't need to tape this, but if you do, twist a thin piece of tape around the straw near the hole and attach the ends to the lid.

What You Need

1 small plastic lid
1 plastic straw   scissors

What You Do

1. Use the scissors to poke a hole in the middle of the lid.

2. Cut the straw in half at an angle. Then push the straw through the hole in the lid.

How It Works

To spin the top, roll the straw between your hands and let the top drop. You can even stand up and let it drop on a smooth floor!

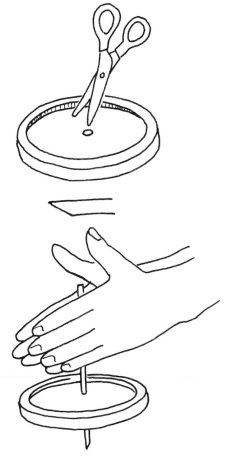

ROUND-ABOUT ART

If you use paper or cardboard plates, you can paint them with fantastic colors and designs. Make a spinning art museum! Experiment with Styrofoam and plastic plates, too.

What You Need

2 picnicware plates
tape
scissors
pencil

What You Do

1. Poke a hole in the middle of each plate with the pencil.

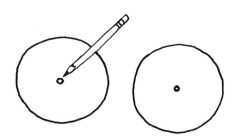

2. Tape the plate rims together, making a hollow space in the middle.

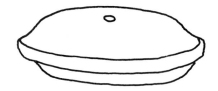

3. Poke the pencil through the holes. The pointed end of the pencil should stick out about an inch.

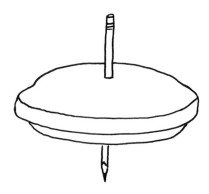

Here's a top that's extra-easy to spin—it's really a spinning ball.

What You Need

1 plastic lid
a quarter (to trace around)
1 Ping-Pong or practice golf ball
scissors   pen   tape

What You Do

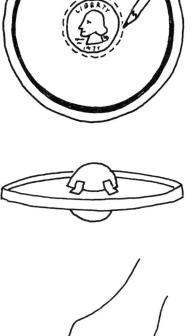

1. Set the quarter in the middle of the lid and trace around it. Cut out the circle.

2. Set the ball on the table and press the lid, upside-down, not quite halfway down onto the ball.

3. Cut eight pieces of tape and stick them up somewhere handy. Use them to tape the ball to the lid on the top and the bottom.

How It Works

The biggest part of the ball is the handle. To spin the top, twist the handle between your thumb and finger, and let the top drop on the small part of the ball.

4. Cut a finger-length piece of tape in half *lengthwise*. Twist one of the tape pieces around the pencil and attach the ends to the top plate. Do the same on the bottom with the second piece of tape.

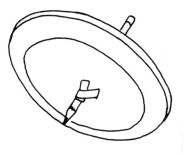

Decorate!

Use some of the ideas on page 9. Paint bright designs on paper or cardboard. Stick things to plastic or Styrofoam. A ring of big, bright dots or a big spiral on a top looks magical when the top spins.

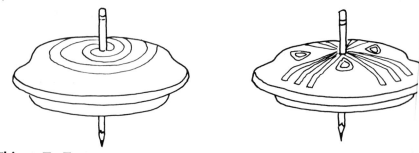

Things To Try

For a wobbly top, make the holes in the plates off-center, but be sure that the bottom hole is exactly beneath the top hole. Or try taping an inch-long piece of straw over the pencil poin

How It Works

To spin the top, roll the pencil between your hands. Then drop it on a table or floor.

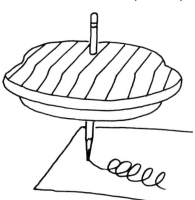

STEADY BETTY

This larger version of Steady Eddie adds weight around the edge to make it spin even longer.

What You Need

1 Styrofoam plate
small ball of modeling clay
a quarter (to trace around)
1 Ping-Pong or practice golf ball
scissors   pen   tape

What You Do

1. Draw a ring around the plate where it begins to curve up. Cut on the line.

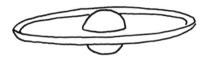

2. Follow the steps for Steady Eddie, using the plate instead of a lid.

3. Roll the clay into a long, thin snake. Press it into the upturned edge of the cut plate.

How It Works

Spin this top the same way as Steady Eddie, using your thumb and finger to give it a whirl.

This fancy outdoor three-wheeler really will come back to you.

What You Need

6 Styrofoam plates
glue   scissors   tape

What You Do

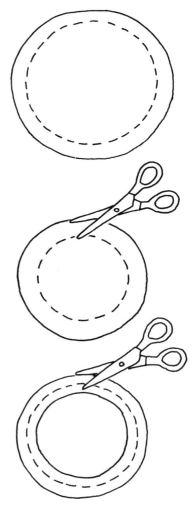

1. Cut the flat center parts out of all six plates. Discard the rims.

2. Cut a ring as wide as your thumb (about 1 inch) from each circle. (Save one of the center circles for later.)

3. Make *three* of the rings a little thinner by cutting a thin strip off the *inside* of each ring.

4. Make a double ring: Glue a fat ring and a thin ring together, matching up the outside edges.

5. Make two more double rings from the remaining fat rings and thin rings.

6. Tape the three double rings together, as in the drawing. Then tape one of the center pieces to the top.

How It Works

To fly the Come Backer, fling it as you would a Frisbee.

SKY CLIMBER

Here's a spinning toy that climbs right up your kite string.

What You Need

1 Styrofoam plate   1 plastic straw
tape   scissors   pencil

What You Do

1. Use a pencil to poke a hole in the middle of the plate. Then cut off the plate's rim.

2. Cut three slots in the circle—only one reaches the middle—as in the drawing. Bend up a flap next to each slot.

3. Cut the straw in half. Tape the straight half in the circle's hole by cutting a finger-length piece of tape in half *lengthwise* and attaching it as shown in the drawing. Tape it on top and bottom.

4. Cut the straw *lengthwise* right where it lines up with the slot in the plate.

How It Works

Slip the Sky Climber onto the kite string through the slit in the straw and watch it shimmy up the string.

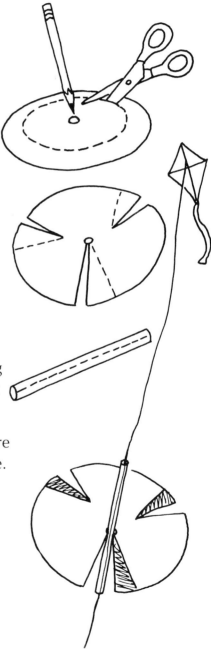

WIND SPINNERS

Wind power twirls the whirling spinners in this group and puffs up the body of a silly Birdbag. All of these wind toys whirl on top of a special, marble-topped Wind Spinner Pole—one pole fits all!

WIND SPINNER POLE

Use this slippery-ended pole to hold any of the spinners in this group out in the wind, or inside in front of a fan.

What You Need

1 stick about as long as your arm:
   a broomstick, ¼-inch dowel, or branch
1 marble (big or little)   plastic tape   scissors

What You Do

1. Wrap a short piece of tape around the lower half of the marble.

2. Set the marble on top of the stick. Then pinch the tape to the stick.

3. Use another piece of tape to hold the first piece of tape to the stick.

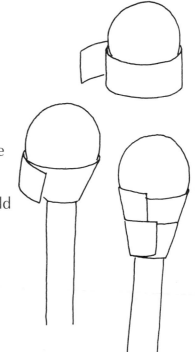

How It Works

To set up the Wind Spinner Pole, use plastic tape to stick it outside in a place where it can catch the wind. Use plenty of tape so it won't fall. Then make one of the Wind Spinners from the next few pages to set on the pole.

WIND SPINNER PARTS

Make some fancy models from these three Wind Spinner parts! Whirl them all on the Wind Spinner Pole.

What You Need

plastic cups
scissors
plastic tape

What You Do

1. To make a *Single-Hole Base:* Use two cups. Cut the bottom out of one cup. Tape the cup to another cup, rim to rim.

2. To make a *Double-Hole Base:* Use two cups. Make a Single-Hole Base (Step 1), *except* cut the bottoms out of both cups.

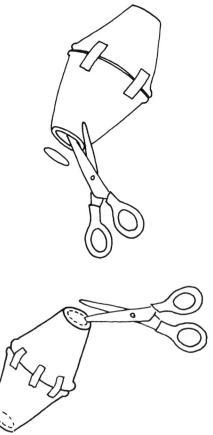

3. To make a *Windcatcher:* Use three
   cups. Lay them on their sides. Tape
   them together, bottom to top of
   side, as in the drawing.

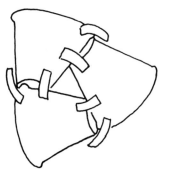

═══════════ MINI WIND SPINNER ═══════════

Here's a nifty spinner made of bright cups—set it on your Wind
Spinner Pole and watch it whirl.

What You Need

1 Single-Hole Base
1 Windcatcher
tape

What You Do

Push the base, hole down, into the
space in the middle of the
Windcatcher. Tape it in place. Now
set it on the Wind Spinner Pole!

═══════ DOUBLE WIND SPINNER ═══════

Make a doubly dizzy toy—just add another Windcatcher!

What You Need

1 Single-Hole Base
1 Double-Hole Base
2 Windcatchers

What You Do

1. Tape the two bases together, matching up two holes.

2. Tape one Windcatcher around the bottom of the Double-Hole Base (the hole end).

3. Untape one of the cups of the other Windcatcher. Retape the Windcatcher around the middle of the joined bases.

How They Work

Set either of the Wind Spinners on the Wind Spinner Pole and watch them whirl in the breeze.

REVOLVING TOTEM POLE

Keep adding Windcatchers and tape on some faces for a wind-powered totem pole.

What You Need

1 Single-Hole Base
several Windcatchers
several Double-Hole Bases
some Styrofoam plates or scraps
ball-point pen   crayons   tape

What You Do

1. Follow Step 1 on page 26, *except* tape together *several* Double-Hole Bases with a Single-Hole Base at the top.

2. Follow Steps 2 and 3, adding as many Windcatchers as you like.

3. To make faces, trace around cup rims on Styrofoam. Draw faces with pen and crayons and cut them out. Tape the faces over about half of the cups.

How It Works

Slip the Wind Spinner Pole through the Totem Pole, all the way to the top. You may need an extra-long pole.

DIZZY WIND FISH

Make a fishy weathervane, so you'll know which way the wind's blowing.

What You Need

1 Double-Hole Base
1 Styrofoam plate
1 Single-Hole Base
1 clamping clothespin
plastic tape   scissors

What You Do

1. Cut a hole in the Double-Hole base where the rims meet. Make the hole big enough to fit over the end of the Single-Hole Base (this is the fish).

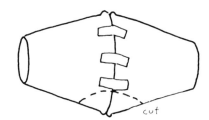

2. Push the closed end of the Single-Hole Base through the hole in the fish. Tape the fish to the base.

3. Cut two eyes in the fish and cut slits for the mouth. At the other end, cut two short slits, one on the top and one on the bottom, for the tail to slide into.

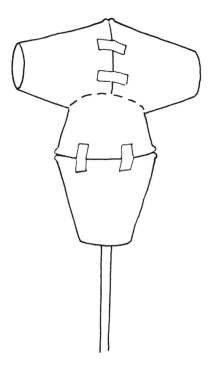

4. Set the end of the fish on the middle of the plate and trace around it. Cut the plate in half. Nest the halves together and cut out the half-circles.

5. Draw a tail like the one in the drawing, a little wider than the cut-out half-circle and going to the edge of the plate. Cut out both pieces at once.

6. Turn one tail piece over and tape the two pieces together so the tail fans out. Slide the tail into the slots in the fish. Tape them well.

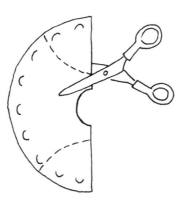

How It Works

Set the Dizzy Wind Fish on your Wind Spinner Pole. Clamp a clothespin pointing north onto the pole, so you'll always know which way the wind is blowing. The Dizzy Wind Fish swims *into* the wind.

BIRDBAG

The Birdbag makes a wonderful puppet—its head twitches in a funny, birdlike way—but it can be a windbag, too! Make it from one of those little crackling sacks many stores use now.

What You Need

1 ⅛-inch dowel
2 Styrofoam plates
1 crackling plastic sack
1 plastic soda pop bottle
paper punch
scissors
tape

What You Do

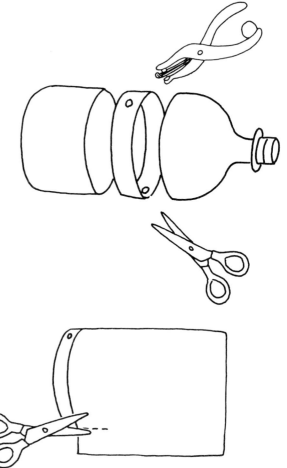

1. Cut a ring from the middle of the bottle. Punch two holes in the ring exactly opposite each other.

2. Pull the edge of the plastic bag around the ring. Pinch it together where it meets at the bottom and snip it there, through both sides of the bag.

3. Lay the bag flat so the snips match up. Draw a headless bird body on the bag between one side and the snips.

4. Cut out the body and tape the loose side edges together, as in the drawing. Then tape the open edge around the ring.

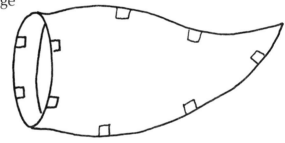

5. Stick the dowel through the ring holes. Wind tape around the dowel so the bird won't slip down.

6. Make a bird head: Draw a circle on one Styrofoam plate. It should be about half the diameter of the plastic ring. Add a big beak and a neck. Cut out the bird head.

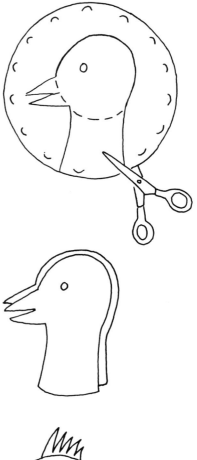

7. Trace the head onto the second plate. Cut out the matching head. Punch eyes in both head pieces with a paper punch.

8. Cut a little fringe from a scrap of sack. Tape it on top of one head. Tape the two head pieces together with the top of the dowel between them.

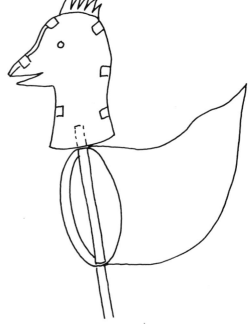

Decorate It!

You can make all kinds of birds, and animals, too, by changing the shape and color of the heads and bodies.

How It Works

Make it a wind toy: Use plenty of tape to attach the Birdbag's dowel to a stick outdoors—the Wind Spinner Pole works fine. The tail of the Birdbag will point in the direction that the wind is blowing, while the wind puffs out the body.

Make it a puppet: Sit down low behind a table and hold the Birdbag above you at table level as you talk for it. You can operate two Birdbags at once—one in each hand.

CRAZY CARS

Once you learn how to make car parts, and how to make the wheels turn, you can build cars and racers that move with surprising speed.

BASIC CRAZY CAR PARTS

The *body* is the car shape.
The *axles* are the straight sticks or bars that hold the *wheels*.
Spacers keep the wheels from banging against the car body.
Stoppers keep the wheels from slipping off the ends of the axles.

TWO WAYS TO MAKE WHEELS TURN

1. Spin the axle.

One way to make wheels turn is to slip the axle inside a bigger tube, or through holes bigger than the axle. Stick the wheels tightly on the end of the axle so the wheels themselves won't turn. The axle and wheels will spin as one piece inside the tube.

Try it! Slide a toothpick through a smaller piece of straw. Stick a carrot slice at each end. Now hold the straw and spin the axle. The wheels spin too!

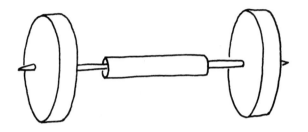

2. Spin the wheels.

The second way to make wheels turn is to slide the axle through a tube or larger hole in the middle of each wheel. The wheels spin on the axle—the axle doesn't turn. (Remember that in Number 1, the wheels and axle turn together.)

Try it! Use the toothpick to poke a hole in the middle of two carrot slices. Poke away enough carrot to make a straw-size hole. Cut two short pieces of straw and push through the hole in each carrot. Slide the wheels on the toothpick. Hold the toothpick with one hand and spin the wheels with the other hand.

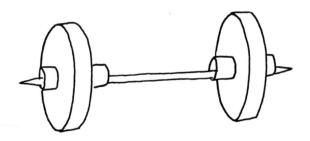

GUMBALL RACER (STREET MODEL)

Right now—before you even start—pop the two "chew glue" gumballs in your mouth and start chewing! (If you're using clay instead, skip this odd beginning.)

What You Need

4 small gumballs   2 round toothpicks
1 plastic straw   1 clamping clothespin
2 small gumballs (for chew glue!) or some modeling clay

What You Do

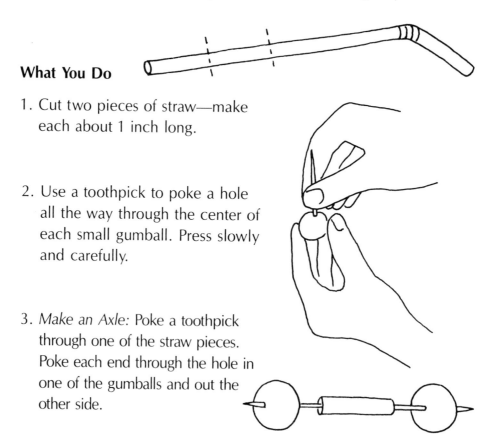

1. Cut two pieces of straw—make each about 1 inch long.

2. Use a toothpick to poke a hole all the way through the center of each small gumball. Press slowly and carefully.

3. *Make an Axle:* Poke a toothpick through one of the straw pieces. Poke each end through the hole in one of the gumballs and out the other side.

4. Repeat Step 3 to make a second axle. *Hint:* You might have to snip the straw pieces to make them shorter if there isn't room for the wheels.

5. Clamp one axle into the front end of the clothespin. Tape the other axle under the clothespin, near the back.

6. Wet your fingers and break off small balls of chewed gum (you are chewing those gumballs, aren't you?). *Or* break off tiny bits of modeling clay. Mold them to the ends of the axles to keep the wheels on.

Be Careful

Once you've made wheels out of gumballs or candy, *don't eat them!*

GUMBALL RACER (SPORTS MODEL)

Use big gumballs like the ones from gumball machines for the back wheels. You can use them in front, too, if you haven't got any small ones.

What You Need

4 gumballs (2 large ones and 2 small ones)
1 toothpick
⅛-inch dowel piece
1 plastic straw
1 clamping clothespin
2 small gumballs for "chew glue," or modeling clay

What You Do

1. Follow Steps 1-3 on page 36 to make one axle for the front. Clamp the axle in the jaws of the clothespin.

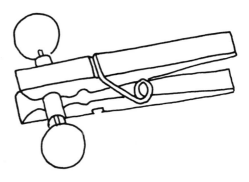

2. Cut two small rings about this wide <———> (about ⅜ inch) from the leftover piece of straw to use for *spacers*.

3. To make the back axle, snap off (or use a scissors to cut) a piece of dowel—make it twice as long as the toothpick that forms the front axle. Poke one end of the dowel piece into a big gumball, and put on a spacer.

4. Poke the axle through the spring hole on the clothespin. Then slip on the other spacer and attach the other large gumball.

5. Wet your fingers. Finish the ends of both axles with tiny balls of chewed gum. *Or* use tiny balls of modeling clay.

CANDY CAR

You can make these just like Gumball Racers, slipping on Life Savers for the wheels. Or you can follow these steps to put wheels on a small box or tin.

What You Need

1 plastic straw
4 Life Saver candies
2 3-inch-long pieces of ⅛-inch dowel
1 small box, like an empty spice tin
some gum (any kind) or modeling clay for stoppers
a discarded plastic bottle cap
tape

What You Do

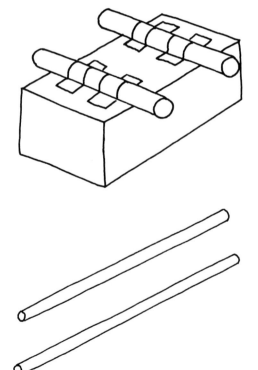

1. Cut two pieces of straw about an inch wider than the box. Tape the straws to one side of the box, as in the drawing.

2. Snap off (or cut with a scissors) two pieces of dowel about this much longer than the straw pieces: <————> (about 1¼ inches longer).

3. Poke a dowel piece through each of the straws. Slide a Lifesaver on each end. Stop the ends with chewed gum or modeling clay.

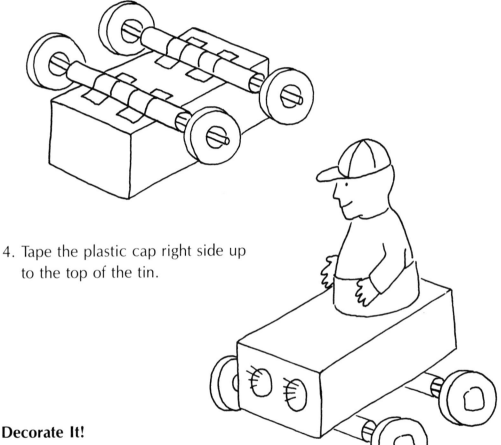

4. Tape the plastic cap right side up to the top of the tin.

Decorate It!

If you like, use modeling clay to mold the shape of a driver onto the plastic cap. Or cut out a paper person and tape that to the cap. You could even glue on a tiny person from your toy box.

Any size buttons make great wheels, as long as the holes are small and quite close together. And you don't need four matched wheels. The two wheels on each axle do need to be the same, but you can use two large buttons and two smaller ones.

What You Need

4 buttons (see note above)
1 clamping clothespin
1 plastic straw
toothpicks (4 for 2-holed buttons, 8 for 4-holed buttons)
bits of clay (optional)
scissors
tape

What You Do

1. Cut the top off the straw just above the bend. The piece will be about an inch long. Cut a second piece that size from the other end of the straw.

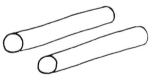

2. Tape the straw pieces onto the clothespin, as shown in the drawing.

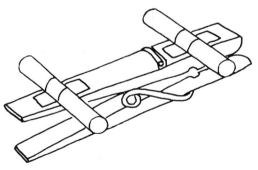

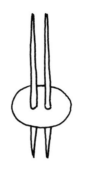

3. Poke toothpicks in all the holes of a button. Slide all the toothpicks stuck in the button through one of the straws taped on the clothespin. Poke the toothpick ends into the holes of another button.

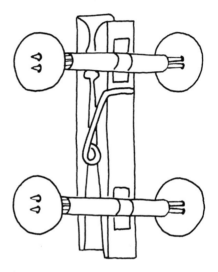

4. Follow Step 3 for the other axle. If you like, mold bits of modeling clay over the axle ends. (The buttons will probably stay on without clay, but you may prefer to cover the toothpick ends.)

CARROT CAR

These cars may not last until tomorrow, but they sure do go today! They're so fast and easy, you can just slice off some new wheels any time you need them.

What You Need

1 carrot
1 clamping clothespin
2 toothpicks
1 plastic straw
knife   scissors
tape

What You Do

Carefully cut slices about ¼ inch wide from the carrot. Then follow the steps for the Button Buggy (page 42), *except* in Step 3, stick *one* toothpick in the middle of a carrot wheel instead of several. Hint: Try to find a carrot that doesn't change size too much from one end to the other.

Wow!

Try making wheels from other raw vegetables, like zucchini, long radishes, round potatoes. For larger cars, use ⅛-inch dowels or Tinker Toy sticks for axles.

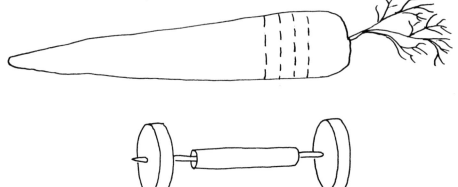

REAL WHEELS

Use Real Wheels to make Crazy Racers (page 47) and other nifty cars in this book. Then make up your own! The foam pipe insulation used here comes in different widths. The hole in the middle also differs. Any size will work, but it's easier to use the kind with a smaller hole.

What You Need

plastic straws
foam pipe insulation
flat pieces of Styrofoam
plastic tape
scissors

What You Do

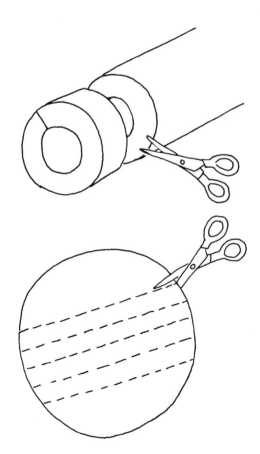

1. *Make tires:* Cut four slices off a foam insulation stick, about this wide <———————> (about 1 inch). Snip through each break place.

2. Cut four Styrofoam strips about the same width as the foam insulation slices; make the strips as long as you can. (Use Styrofoam egg carton tops, meat trays, or plate middles.)

3. Cut a straw into four equal pieces.

4. *Make the wheel:* Tape one end of a Styrofoam strip to the middle of a straw piece. Roll the Styrofoam tightly around the straw. Tape the end down. (Be gentle. If the strip breaks, just tape the broken end down and start another strip on top of it.)

5. Fit the Styro-straw inside a wheel. It should fit tightly. If it doesn't, wrap more Stryofoam strips around the straw until you get a snug fit.

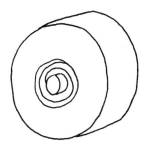

6. Tape the wheel closed, going all the way around the "tire."

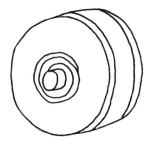

7. Follow Steps 4-6 to make three more wheels.

CRAZY RACER

These racers are easy to handle, simple to make, and they perform beautifully. On top of all that, they look fantastic!

What You Need

4 Real Wheels (page 45)
foam pipe insulation
1 ⅛-inch dowel
scraps of Styrofoam or plastic soda pop bottles
plastic tape
scissors

What You Do

1. Make four Real Wheels (page 45).

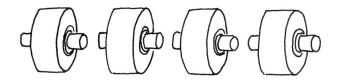

2. Make washers: From scraps of Styrofoam or plastic, cut eight penny-size circles. Punch a hole in the middle of each one with a pencil or scissors.

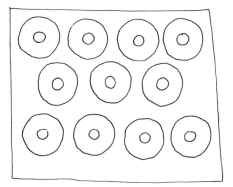

3. Cut off a piece of foam pipe insulation about as long as your hand (6 inches or so).

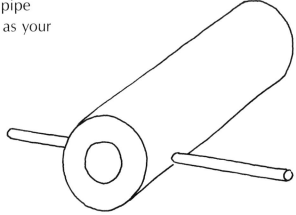

4. Measure the axles: Push the dowel through the insulation near one end. Slide a wheel on each end of the dowel. Adjust the dowel so the wheels spin freely. Then break or cut the dowel off to the right length.

5. Break off or cut another dowel piece the same size.

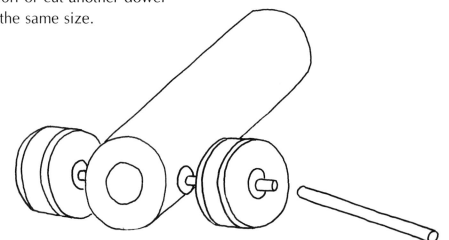

6. Assemble the car: Poke a dowel
   through the foam near each end.
   Make them the same distance
   from the floor, and exactly
   parallel to one another.

7. Slide on the parts for each wheel
   in this order: washer—wheel—washer.
   Wind tape or a tiny strip of Styrofoam
   and tape around the end of the dowel
   to keep the wheel on. Do the same for
   the other three wheels.

SKATEBOARD CAR

Use the materials for the Crazy Racer (page 47), but instead of using pipe insulation for the body, cut a skateboard shape from a Styrofoam plate.

What You Do

1. Cut a skateboard shape from the plate.

2. String two Real Wheels and their washers on a dowel (axle) and tape the ends. Tape the axle to the skateboard, making sure it's on straight.

3. Do the same with the second axle and the other set of wheels and washers.

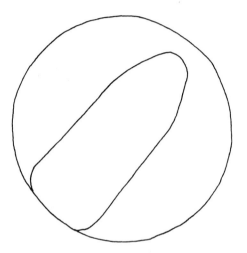

CUP CAR

Fast food cups for this car's body make a really racy model.

What You Need

4 Real Wheels (page 45)
1 ⅛-inch dowel
plastic tape
2 picnicware cups   scissors
scraps of Styrofoam or plastic soda pop bottles

What You Do

1. Poke the dowel through one of the cups and out again near the bottom to make axle holes. Keep the axle straight and fairly low.

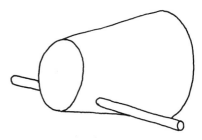

2. Leave enough room on each side of the axle to hold a wheel plus tape on the ends. Snap off the dowel. Pull the axle out and snap off a second piece of dowel the same size.

3. Set the second cup inside the first cup. Mark the holes and punch them with a dowel piece. Then take the cups apart again.

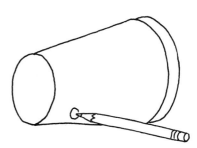

4. Put the axles through the holes.
   Tape the rims of the cups
   together so the axles are even.

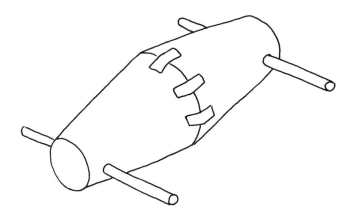

5. Cut eight penny-sized circles
   from Styrofoam or picnicware
   scraps. Then follow Step 7 for the
   Crazy Racer (page 49) to put on
   the wheels.

POWER PACK

This simple balloon-and-straw assembly can shoot a lightweight Real Wheel car across a slick kitchen floor!

What You Need

scissors
plastic tape
1 plastic straw
1 round balloon

What You Do

1. Cut the lip off the balloon.

2. Cut the straw in half.

3. Stick the straw into the balloon and tape it in place. If air leaks out when you blow through the straw, use some more tape.

4. Tape the straw to the top of a Crazy Car so the straw sticks out the back like a muffler.

How It Works

Blow up the balloon through the straw, pinch the straw closed, and set the car down. Then let go and watch it *move!*

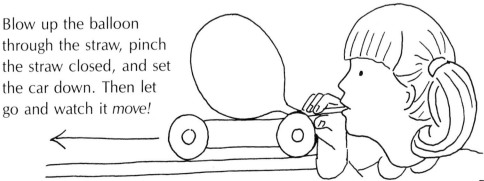

BALLOON-POWERED GO-CART

You can make this Go-Cart without the balloon if you want to.

What You Need

1 ⅛-inch dowel
1 Styrofoam plate
3 Real Wheels (page 45)
1 Power Pack (page 53)
6 washers (penny-size circles cut from Styrofoam)
plastic tape
scissors

What You Do

1. On the plate, draw a Go-Cart body like the one in the drawing. Use the rim for one end, and make a big "U" at the other. Cut it out.

2. Snap off a piece of dowel to fit the flat front end. Put a washer-wheel-washer on the center of the dowel. Then tape the dowel to the front end.

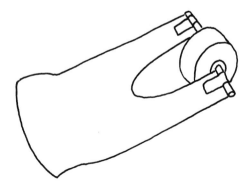

3. Snap off a dowel piece for a rear axle; make sure to leave room for two wheels plus tape or clay on the ends. Tape the axle under the back end just before it curves up.

4. Slide a washer-wheel-washer on each end of the axle as in the drawing. Wind tape at the ends or mold on bits of clay.

5. Punch a hole in the tilted back end. Poke the Power Pack straw through so it sticks out like a muffler. Tape it in place.

How It Works

Blow the balloon up, pinch the straw, set the Go-Cart on the floor, and *let go!*

The basic directions here are for Styrofoam plate wheels. But you can use *any* picnicware plates or bowls; see the special directions on page 57.

What You Need

16 Styrofoam plates (4 for each wheel)
stapler
plastic tape

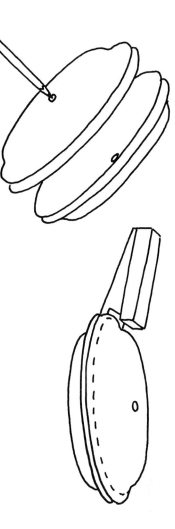

What You Do

1. Stack one plate inside another to make a double-thick plate. Then make another double-thick plate with two more. Poke a hole in the middle of each set.

2. Staple or tape the rims of the plate sets together, as in the drawing, so they make a fat wheel.

3. Run a long piece of tape around the edge and pinch it in place.

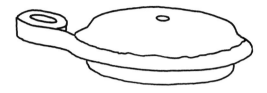

Using other picnicware

If you have cardboard, paper, or plastic picnicware, simply use a different number of plates to make four wheels:

8 cardboard plates: use 2 plates per wheel;

8 plastic plates: use 2 plates per wheel;

24 thin paper plates: use 6 plates per wheel.

BOX CAR

You can make a variation of this car from a small box—with smaller wheels, of course. If you do, you can use thinner dowels.

What You Need

4 Big Wheels (page 56)
1 ¼-inch dowel (or ⅛-inch)
a shoebox or something like it
a Styrofoam egg carton or a plastic straw

What You Do

1. Make holes exactly across from each other in the bottom corners of each long side of the box (four holes in all).

2. Poke a dowel through one set of holes. Hold it with four fingers at the end of the dowel and four more on the other side. Break the axle off where your fingers end.

3. Break off another piece of dowel the same size for the second axle.

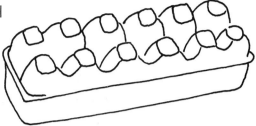

4. To make spacers, cut out four cups from the egg carton. Use a pencil to punch a hole in the bottom of each cup. Or cut four 1-inch pieces from a straw.

5. Tape one end of an axle. Slide on a wheel and then a spacer (egg carton or straw). Poke the axle through a set of holes in the box.

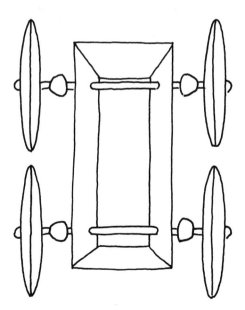

6. Slide on another spacer and wheel. Tape the end. Be sure the wheels can move easily.

7. Follow Steps 5-6 for the other axle.

8. Put on the boxtop and roll! Or bend the boxtop up at one end (first snip the rim in the same place on each side).

Hint: You can use ⅛-inch dowels but they sometimes snap under the weight of bigger toys. Tinker Toys are exactly the right size for axles if you don't have ¼-inch dowels. Some bamboo plant stakes work, too.

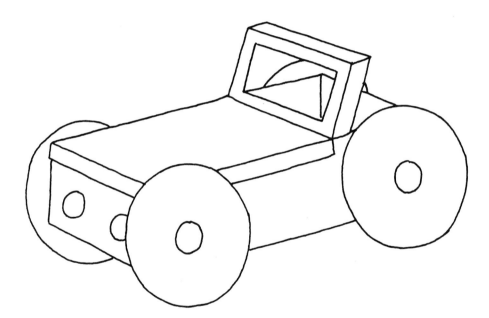

BOTTLE MODEL

This racy-looking number is a copy of the Box Car (page 58)—except that you use a 2-liter plastic soda pop bottle instead of the box! Use a scissors to poke the holes.

What You Do

Follow the directions for the Box Car on pages 58-59. Make the front wheels smaller for a jazzy look.

ROCKET CAR

This car is the same as the Box Car (page 58), *except* you use two big fast food cups instead of the shoebox. If you can, make the front wheels smaller than the back ones.

What You Do

1. Poke the dowel through one of the cups and out again near the bottom to make axle holes. Keep the axle straight and fairly low. Do the same with the second cup.

2. Tape the cups together rim to rim, keeping the axle holes even.

3. Follow the Steps 2-7 for the Box Car on page 58; if you're using two small wheels, put those in front.

INVENT YOUR OWN CARS AND RACERS

Now that you can make wheels and axles, you can make cars from all sorts of things. Here are some ideas for car parts.

Things that make good car bodies:

clamping clothespins	empty spice tins
empty boxes	plastic hair rollers
plastic soda pop bottles	foam pipe insulation
empty match boxes	picnicware and fast food cups
flat Styrofoam shapes	plastic sponges and foam

wooden blocks and some plastic building blocks

Things that make good wheels:

Life Savers	raw round vegetable slices
gumballs	metal washers
buttons	spools
foam pipe insulation	picnicware bowls and plates

Things that make good axles:

toothpicks	wooden dowels
Tinker Toy sticks	straight bush branches
plastic straws	pencils
pick-up sticks	bamboo plant stakes

Things that make good spacers:

slices of plastic straw	cups cut out of egg cartons
restaurant plastic creamer cups	

Things that make good washers:

Punch a hole in the middle of each circle cut from:

Styrofoam egg cartons   plastic picnicware
Styrofoam meat trays   plastic soda pop bottles
Styrofoam picnicware

Things that make good wheel caps:

Keep the wheels on with one of these:

chewed gum   modeling clay
rolled tape   rolled and taped Styrofoam strip

You may not have noticed, but while you've been transforming plates and balloons and other things into toys, you've been transformed too. You've turned into a mechanic, an engineer, a scientist, an artist, and even a musician! You may have been a student, making something for a classroom project, or a teacher, showing someone else how to make a toy like yours. Best of all, you've become an inventor, creating the most exciting thing of all—your own fun!